the nature of God

Glen,

May you enjoy and embrace Graham's insights into God and able to experience Him in new ways.

Your friend,

Jon Hupfod

an
interactive
journal

book three
being with God series

the nature of God

*Upgrading your image of God and
who He wants to be for you*

Graham Cooke

Sovereign World

Sovereign World Ltd
PO Box 777
Tonbridge
Kent TN11 0ZS
England

Requests for information should be addressed to:
Graham Cooke
PO Box 91
Southampton
SO15 5ZE, United Kingdom
Website: http://www.grahamcooke.com

ISBN 1 85240 359 4

Cover design by CCD, www.ccdgroup.co.uk
Typeset by CRB Associates, Reepham, Norfolk
Printed in the United States of America

dedication

There is only one Person I can dedicate this book to –
the Holy Spirit. I am constantly amazed at His wisdom,
revelation, and power in my life. I love His dedication
to, and His passion for, the Lord Jesus Christ. The way
He reveals the Son to me has changed my life. His
physical, emotional, mental, and spiritual
representation of the Father to me has continuously
made me more excited and in awe of the great love of
God for me.

acknowledgements

Heather, Ben with Sioux, Seth and Yvonne and of course, Sophie: What a great, wacky family we are ... I love it!

Carole Shiers, my personal assistant and faithful ministry partner for many, many years: thank you.

To the respective churches in Southampton (UK) and Vacaville (USA) which I call home: Thank you, especially to my leaders, Billy and Caroline Kennedy (UK) and David and Deborah Crone (USA) for including us and being our friends.

To Tim and Darlene Dickerson who graciously provide a home, support, and, above all, true, loving friendship that withholds nothing: What a great blessing our relationship is for me and my family.

Finally, to Jordan Bateman, thank you for helping me enormously with the journal project, and to Tim Pettingale, my publisher and friend, whose passion for books and the written word is only outdone by his love for Jesus.

introduction

I strongly believe that a major shift is coming in the western church. We are embarking on a time when the church will stop explaining who God is and begin proclaiming His nature, His acts, and His glory.

God doesn't need to be explained, He needs to be lauded. He needs to be proclaimed and worshipped. He needs people who are going to shout out who He really is, and what He's really like. His Good News is the best news of all. In a world consumed by heartache, sin, pain, and bad news, Christians can offer the Good News of who God really is.

Many people – Christian and pre-Christian – have a wrong view of God. They see Him in a number of ways, none of which properly reflect the majesty of His presence. It's important that we capture the image that God wants to sow into our heart. What we think about God is the single most important thing in our spiritual journey. Our image of God will drive every single part of our life and declare how we show up in the world. Do we live a life of faith, boldness and conviction? If we don't, we need to examine our perception of God.

People who are doubtful about what God wants to do need to strongly upgrade their image of Him. God wants us to be confident in Him, and in His love for us.

I wonder how many of us have lost – or maybe never had – that intimate knowledge of God as our Father. He must be the most important thing in our world. We're shaped, emotionally and spiritually, by the image of God we carry in our hearts and minds. He loves us. He enjoys us. He is deeply personal with us, as well as being the Almighty God of the entire universe.

God is paradoxical – He is faithful to me even when I am not faithful to Him. His love and faithfulness must win our hearts to a deeper level in Him.

Graham Cooke
March 2003

the nature of God

Whenever we move into a new spiritual dimension of our calling and our ministry, we must take the time to upgrade our relationship with God. Our calling comes at different levels at different times; it is a progressive journey of discovery. When God takes us into the next phase of our calling, our relationship with Him must also change.

Throughout our lives, we will enter into many different phases and experiences. It might be a marriage or the birth of a child, a significant work promotion, a new responsibility, a new ministry, or any other type of change. In seasons like that, we must take the time to upgrade our peace and rest in the Lord. If we enter a new situation without fully immersing ourselves in the stillness of God, we will live on our adrenaline and not out of our spirit. This power boost may seem sufficient at the moment, but for every adrenaline high, there is also an adrenaline low. We cannot sustain that needed adrenaline rush over the long term. Eventually, our energy will wither away and the new season will overwhelm us. We must learn to live in a place of rest in the spirit.

Every experience of God, even resting in Him, should enable us to see Him in a different light. Therefore, we need to constantly re-evaluate our relationship with Him and take a deeper look at our walk with Him. We must critically examine our current picture of God and determine whether it is strong enough for the next stage of our life and call. If it's not, the stress that we will experience will put pressure on us to quit or scale down our involvement in the new seasons of our lives. That same battle fatigue causes us to shrink back from the challenges facing us. Exhausted, we will talk ourselves out of taking the risks necessary to advance the Kingdom of God. God has given us the ability to live under His wing – we must recognize that we exist within the safety of His love and grace, and not on our own.

> "The law of the LORD is perfect, converting the soul."
> Psalm 19:7

I cannot emphasize this enough – every time we are led into a new phase of our journey, we must take time to upgrade our image of God. We can travel confidently into any new experience, no matter how challenging or difficult, in our relationship with Him. God wants to build up your confidence right now, taking it to a whole new dimension.

When we enter a new season it is important to ask

ourselves relevant questions regarding its likely impact on all of our relationships and current responsibilities. Present levels of stress will need to be adjusted in the light of a deeper peace and rest that will be required on the next leg of the journey.

Change is much better if it is gradual over time rather than a large overwhelming transformation requiring immediate extensive attention. The two questions required of us in a consistent basis are found in Acts 2, verses 12 and 37:

- ▶ What does this mean?
- ▶ What must we do?

How will these adjustments affect our relationship with God and one another? How will this new season deepen my love, joy and peace in the Holy Spirit?

We need to gain a fresh and more powerful image of the nature of God. We need to practice our peace and our patience so that we can break through, in harmony with others, into a new dimension of the Spirit.

Moses gets upgraded

Moses' relationship with God is a strong example of how a person's view of the Lord can be upgraded during specific seasons of life. In Exodus 3, the man is toiling in the wilderness, far from the glory of God and completely removed from his former life as a prince in

Egypt. He wasn't even tending his own flock of sheep –
he was working for his father-in-law. Still, God had a
plan for Moses' life, and a desire to see the lonely
shepherd upgrade his image of who God wanted to be
for him. This desire brought Moses to the burning bush,
where God could speak to Moses about his future,
Israel's deliverance, and His own nature. *"I AM Who
I AM,"* God said in Exodus 3:14,
completely shifting Moses' view of God.
This perception changed Moses' life,
turning the stuttering murderer into
Israel's deliverer. It was a powerful
calling on his life which had to be
accompanied by an upgrade in his relationship with
God.

> "You prepare a table before me in the presence of my enemies; You anoint my head with oil; my cup runs over."
> Psalm 23:5

After fulfilling that call and leading Israel out of
Egypt, Moses' friendship with God was again upgraded
as his calling further increased:

> *"Then the LORD said to Moses, 'Depart and go up
> from here, you and the people whom you have
> brought out of the land of Egypt, to the land of
> which I swore to Abraham, Isaac, and Jacob,
> saying, "To your descendants I will give it."
> And I will send My Angel before you, and I will
> drive out the Canaanite and the Amorite and the
> Hittite and the Perizzite and the Hivite and the
> Jebusite. Go up to a land flowing with milk and*

honey; for I will not go up in your midst, lest I consume you on the way, for you are a stiff-necked people.'

And when the people heard this bad news, they mourned, and no one put on his ornaments. For the LORD had said to Moses, 'Say to the children of Israel, "You are a stiff-necked people. I could come up into your midst in one moment and consume you. Now therefore, take off your ornaments, that I may know what to do to you."' So the children of Israel stripped themselves of their ornaments by Mount Horeb." (Exodus 33:1–6)

Moses' call had changed. In Exodus 3, it was primarily about bringing Israel out of bondage and oppression – Moses was a deliverer. Now, in Exodus 33, it wasn't about bringing people out; it was about taking people in. His call was now to bring Israel into its land of promise. He had to be consumed with inheritance, not deliverance. And whenever a call changes, your relationship with God must change first.

> "Fear not, for I am with you; be not dismayed, for I am your God. I will strengthen you, yes, I will help you, I will uphold you with My righteous right hand."
> Isaiah 41:10

If there was one man who could have been content with where his relationship with God sat, it was Moses. In Exodus 33:7–11, we are given a taste of how strong that bond was:

"Moses took his tent and pitched it outside the camp, far from the camp, and called it the tabernacle of meeting. And it came to pass that everyone who sought the LORD went out to the tabernacle of meeting which was outside the camp. So it was, whenever Moses went out to the tabernacle, that all the people rose, and each man stood at his tent door and watched Moses until he had gone into the tabernacle. And it came to pass, when Moses entered the tabernacle, that the pillar of cloud descended and stood at the door of the tabernacle, and the LORD talked with Moses. All the people saw the pillar of cloud standing at the tabernacle door, and all the people rose and worshipped, each man in his tent door. So the LORD spoke to Moses face to face, as a man speaks to his friend. And he would return to the camp, but his servant Joshua the son of Nun, a young man, did not depart from the tabernacle."

"Joshua the son of Nun, a young man, did not depart from the tabernacle." I'm pretty sure I wouldn't either! All of Israel would watch as their leader went to the meeting place and the cloud came down upon the tent. It was an awesome sight, and a strong testimony to Moses' relationship with God: "So the LORD spoke to Moses face to face, as a man speaks to his friend." Despite all of this favor Moses had, it was time for another upgrade in his relationship with God. He needed an even deeper relationship because the call on his life had been changed so dramatically – the burning bush and tent of meeting were no longer enough. In preparation for the stress and pressure of the next big thing, Moses had to have his relationship with the Lord upgraded. And Moses wanted that upgrade badly.

God took Moses and put him in a specific place of longing and desire for the one thing God really wanted to give him. In Heaven, there was a conversation over Moses' life amongst the Father, the Son and the Holy Spirit. "Look at Moses," the Trinity said. "He's at a new place in his life. What is it I want to do for him? Well, I want to show him who I really am. I want to upgrade his picture of Me. What I'll do is get him to ask Me a question, so he can get a picture of Me that will sustain him through everything he is going to have to go through. I want to show him My glory, My supremacy, and My sovereignty."

That day in the Tent of Meeting, God maneuvered Moses into a corner where the prophet realized he had favor from the Lord to ask anything. God wasn't saying no to Moses at this point, so he decided to push everything as far as he could. Eventually, Moses asked the question God had been waiting for – "Please, show me Your glory," Moses asked in Exodus 33:18. Those five words were exactly what God wanted to hear. It's as if He said, "What a great idea! Let's do that!" We can read the rest of the account in Exodus 33:19–23:

> *"But He said, 'You cannot see My face; for no man shall see Me, and live.' And the LORD said, 'Here is a place by Me, and you shall stand on the rock. So it shall be, while My glory passes by, that I will put you in the cleft of the rock, and will cover you with My hand while I pass by. Then I will take away My hand, and you shall see My back; but My face shall not be seen.'"*

"I want you to be with Me," the Lord basically told Moses, "but My glory would incinerate you. Instead, I'll protect you in the cleft of this rock and you will be able to see My back." God arranged the entire scenario to put Moses right where He wanted him, all because God hungered to show him something he had never seen before. And then God walked past him. I can't even imagine this; it's beyond our ability to fathom.

> "Therefore the LORD will wait, that He may be gracious to you; and therefore He will be exalted, that He may have mercy on you. For the LORD is a God of justice; blessed are all those who wait for Him."
> Isaiah 30:18

Moses not only got to see the back of Almighty God, he got to hear Him proclaim truth about Himself, as we read in Exodus 34:6:

> *"The LORD, the LORD God, merciful and gracious, longsuffering, and abounding in goodness and*

truth, keeping mercy for thousands, forgiving iniquity and transgression and sin, by no means clearing the guilty, visiting the iniquity of the fathers upon the children and the children's children to the third and the fourth generation.''

Whenever the Lord talks about Himself, take serious note of what He is saying.

mission impossible?

God has not called us to do what seems possible, reasonable or normally attainable; He has called us to do the impossible. He wants us to stretch beyond our ability, our faith, and our capacity to reason. He wants us to do more than we could ever imagine or dream. If you are reading this and think that your call is attainable, it's time for an upgrade. Christians are not supposed to be doing what is possible. We're supposed to be doing what is impossible and outrageous. To accomplish our calling, we must put our hand in the hand of God, learning to be completely dependent on the Holy Spirit for everything.

We have not truly learned to be dependent on the Holy Spirit in every facet of our lives – we continually try to make our own way. One of the common charismatic prayers I have come to dislike is "Holy Spirit, come." For me, the prayer is not "Holy Spirit, come," but "Lord, take not your Holy Spirit from me." The Holy Spirit is ever-present, so our whole approach should be to create a life where He is free to work. "Do what You want to do and let us know what that is," must become our prayer. In our relationship with God, we must not do anything that will upset our delicate balance with Him. Our task is to preserve our relationship with Him, not have to seek one because we have not walked with Him properly.

When the Lord tells us to seek Him it is for one of two reasons. Firstly because we are backslidden or have become indolent in our walk and must recover the ground of our relationship with Him. Secondly it is because we are coming into a new season and must take the time to develop a deeper expression of God in our hearts. In this context, He seeks us first to establish His desire in us. Our job is to make Him welcome and do the things which keep the Holy Spirit with us.

"God is with the generation of the righteous."
Psalm 14:5

That balance hinges on our obedience. *"You are My friends if you do whatever I command you,"* Jesus said in John 15:14. A relationship with God depends on our obedience to Him. If we heed His commands, we will abide in His love. Obedience is a key to the presence of God – learning to simply rest and stay in God is a spiritual discipline.

Forgiven

My beloved one.

How can you be depressed by your own sinfulness when the wonders and joys of my mercy are freely available?

Dear one, why be nailed by the enemy when the keys of my unfettered grace can open every prison in your life?

Why be subject to the relentless condemnation of the evil one when the love of the one who is Almighty is yours to delight in?

Do you not know that the enemy is defeated?

Do you not appreciate that you are endlessly forgiven?

I am going to peel away this part of your life and expose the grace that is freely available. I am not obsessed by sin, I have dealt with it by judging Christ.

I am obsessed by you loving my grace, and experiencing the joy of my life within your heart.

You have always been forgiven. You must learn to forgive yourself.

Become as gracious as your God. Do not nail other people (even if you legitimately can), but be endlessly forgiving. They who are forgiven much also love much.

Enjoy forgiveness; revel in it! I am not disillusioned with you, for I never had any illusions about you.

I have always understood who you are and the struggles you face.

Why would I not love you, since I am love itself?

Live as one not condemned, but released.

Then take the key of my grace and unlock the prison door of as many captives as you can find.

Forgiveness grows when it is employed.

new revelation

Many of us are coming into a new thing right now, with a new call or new responsibilities or a new role. What does it mean for you this year? What does it mean for your relationship with God?

In this upgrade, God wants to declare something else to you about Himself. You see, God always wants to be something significant for us. The question shouldn't be, "Why is this happening to me?" The "why" question is never answered on earth. It is the wrong question. It should be, "What is it that God wants to be for me now that He couldn't be at any other time, in any other way?" What is it about your current situation that is designed to bring you into a deeper relationship with God? Every circumstance in our life is about that – difficulty and blessing. If you're being severely challenged right now, God wants to be something for you. If you're walking in incredible favor and transformation, He's showing you His nature in that, as well.

God wants to declare what He is becoming to you. Like Moses, you have fresh favor to ask Him to go deeper. God is the sneakiest Person on the planet. You cannot have a desire for Him that is unmatched by His desire for you. In fact, if you really want to know where you are with God, check out what is in your own heart. What are you sighing about right now? During those times you sit in the presence of God and your heart sighs for Him, what is it you are sighing for? Understand that your sigh originated in His heart. It is His longing for you, reaching out to you!

> "However, when He, the Spirit of truth, has come, He will guide you into all truth; for He will not speak on His own authority, but whatever He hears He will speak; and He will tell you things to come."
> John 16:13

When you understand what it is your spirit is sighing for, you will understand exactly what He wants to do. You cannot have a desire or longing for God that He did not put there. Your heart for Him is simply a reflection of His heart for you; God has us longing for the things He most wants to give us.

a purposeful God

When God showed Moses His glory, it was not a spontaneous act. God was being purposeful with His servant; He had this planned for quite a while. It was part of His step-by-step plan to reveal Himself to Moses.

What is the nature of your current request of God? In your relationship with Him, what are you asking for? What is the Holy Spirit doing in your life right now? What is He provoking in you? What are you longing for? These are questions you must think through and meditate on, because God's plan for the next phase of your call is already in action. He has been purposeful with you from the very beginning.

a call to leadership

This purposefulness is especially difficult for church leaders to grasp, but it is absolutely vital to the health of the Kingdom that leaders get a hold of it. When Moses went to meet with the Lord, all of Israel could see it. They knew he had a deep relationship with God, and this inspired them.

I love to see leaders on their faces worshipping in a meeting. I believe, having been in thousands of churches and meetings over my life, that the quality of a body's worship is directly dependent upon the observable quality of the relationship the body's leaders have with God. If they are on their faces before Him, the body is too. If they are sitting in the front row of the church, flipping through their Bibles and acting bored, it is impossible to expect the rest of the house to be engaged with God. If anyone is going to be lost in worship, it has to be leadership. We must see our leaders worshipping God.

> "Give to the Lord the glory due His name; bring an offering, and come before Him. Oh, worship the Lord in the beauty of holiness!"
> 1 Chronicles 16:29

I truly believe that there is no place for burnout in the church. People who burnout in ministry haven't properly upgraded their relationship with God. If you don't take care of your relationship with God, your ministry actually becomes a focal point and you fall into idolatry. What you think about most is what you love the most. If you are consumed with your ministry, your leadership, your church, your role, or whatever else, and you are not consumed by who God is for you, you're headed into idolatry. And burnout looms around the corner. Therefore, God must be foremost in our hearts.

intimacy and favour

When God is cemented at the fore of our hearts, we see our relationship with Him deepen in ways we never thought possible. There is a place in the Holy Spirit set aside for every one of us where we can make the enemy tired, depressed, weary, confused, and exasperated. It's a place where our relationship with God has a profound effect on the enemy and the people we live amongst. What we think about God can shatter the hold of darkness on our friends and family. Our intimacy with God should be our most intimidating weapon against the enemy. We have all seen people trying to operate in authority when they just don't have it – it's painful to see. As well-trained charismatic Christians, we think getting louder is how we should try to take authority. But our authority comes out of who we are in Christ, and our capacity to intimidate the enemy comes out of our intimacy with God.

The Lord's favor is available to every single one of us. It's favor to understand God, to go to a deeper

> "The LORD is my strength and song, and He has become my salvation; He is my God, and I will praise Him; my father's God, and I will exalt Him."
> Exodus 15:2

level in Him, and to upgrade our vision and image of who God is for us. It's part of coming into the next phase of accomplishing the impossible. It's a necessary revelation of who God is. It's amazing how God works. When you move into a deeper place with God, the stress that flows out of your life and ministry actually cements and establishes your upgraded relationship with Him.

The antidote to stress and crisis is upgrading our fellowship with God. I know there are different things on my agenda this year related to my call, and I know that makes me vulnerable. I'm going to have to wade through some stuff about myself, fight my feelings of inadequacy, and battle insecurity. I'm confident where I am right now, but when God increases the call in my life, I know I have to go back to working through all of those issues again. I have to translate my weaknesses into joyful vulnerability. I must upgrade my relationship with Him, becoming more intimate than ever before.

What distinguishes a true believer, someone who is walking in the spirit as opposed to their soul – mind, will and emotions – is the favor that ties into our intimacy with God. In Exodus 33:15–16, Moses made it clear what he needed from the Lord during the next season of his life:

"If Your Presence does not go with us, do not bring us up from here. For how then will it be known that Your people and I have found grace in Your sight, except You go with us? So we shall be separate, Your people and I, from all the people who are upon the face of the earth."

Favor comes from having the presence of God traveling with us. We know we carry that favor when He lives among us. We are people of His presence; we must learn how to abide in it. We must learn how to rest, dwell, and remain in God's arms.

our attention span

Learning to be still is difficult in a world dedicated to grabbing our attention. I remember years ago when my wife and children asked me to get a dog. I didn't need to be prophetic to know this was going to end in trouble for me. But when the whole family aligns against you, it's impossible to resist, so, against my better judgment, we got this beast. It was just a fur ball and, to be honest, you couldn't tell which end was which.

Naturally, there had been promises made beforehand: Don't worry, Dad, I'll feed it, I'll walk it, I'll look after it. Those commitments lasted about three-and-a-half weeks. Eventually, this thing became an evil influence in our house. It pounced everywhere. We were living in the country then, and there were horse riding stables down the road. Our dog would squeeze under the fence, jump on a horse's back, and ride them around the field.

I think the stupid animal was a cross between a stunt man and Superman.

> "I, even I, am He who comforts you. Who are you that you should be afraid of a man who will die, and of the son of a man who will be made like grass?"
> Isaiah 51:12

Anyway, I resolved to teach this beast to sit, even if it killed me. It took me two full months – the animal just wouldn't take me seriously. It had the attention span of a gnat. Sit, sit, sit, sit, I would say. Eventually, wonder of wonders, it sat. And then, after a few more sessions, it sat and stayed for me. I considered it a miracle on the level of Moses parting the Red Sea.

A few months later, I was on a tour of Malaysia and the Philippines. The spiritual warfare was incredible; I remember being at one place where we had to walk through hundreds of Islamic people throwing things and spitting at us. Everyone in the conference was really nervous, as windows were being broken and all sorts of other things were happening.

In my spirit, I heard God telling me to "sit, stay." Where had I heard that before? In this warfare situation, I was supposed to learn about peace and rest. The Lord told me that He wasn't going to take care of things out there until I took care of things in my own heart. What was happening out there was designed to teach me to be at peace and at rest in the room. God had given me a place in Christ where He wanted me to sit and stay; that whole tour of Asia was one battle after another, teaching me how to abide, rest and remain in God.

being established in Christ

The Holy Spirit has come to establish us in Christ. Conversely, the enemy has come to take us out of who we are in Christ. The Holy Spirit wants to establish our standing. The enemy wants to bring us into the state of seeing ourselves as powerless, helpless and buried under pressure; but we must see ourselves as who we are in Jesus. The Holy Spirit is working to establish us in Christ and we have to learn how to abide there. We must not be moved.

Our goal, then, is to cooperate with the Holy Spirit and stay with Him in this process. We can then learn how to live in peace, and how to remain in God. The Prince of Peace is more than a title, it is part of God's nature which He wants to implant in us.

If we cannot learn that lesson, we will not survive on the battlefield. Breakthroughs don't come without a fight. There is a call to battle on every one of us. What precedes the fight is increasing our skill in battle by learning the ability to see God as our refuge and fortress. He is our high tower, our righteous One; in

Him, we are safe. We must learn to live in a place where God is supreme.

Eventually, we learn to trust in the nature of God. I believe that God still wants to protect us in the cleft of a rock, and allow His goodness to pass before us. He wants us to see His lovingkindness in our lives. In my own relationship with God, I have found Him to be a paradox – two apparently conflicting ideas contained in the same truth. He is the kindest and happiest person I have ever met; a gentle Father, always smiling, always gracious, always good, and always restful. In His presence, there is joy and peace. At the same time, He is the most powerful being in the universe – He is the Prince of Peace (Isaiah 9:6), and a Man of War (Exodus 15:3).

> "Do not be afraid, Abram. I am your shield, your exceedingly great reward."
> Genesis 15:1

We only need a refuge when we come under attack; we must learn where that safe place is and go there when we're in trouble. This isn't rocket science or quantum physics, it is common sense. God is our secret place, so hidden that the enemy can't even get into the neighborhood.

God is generous, consistent, unchangeable, eternal, everlasting, and always the same. He never gets disillusioned with us; He never had any illusions about us in the first place. He knew exactly what He was taking on with us and we can't surprise Him. He knows everything about us – He's seen the worst of us. In fact, the very moment we were at our worst was the day we realized He had chosen us and was calling us back to Him.

Before Moses proclaimed God's name in Exodus 33–34, he talked about God's compassion. God loves being compassionate. He knows that He is the most compassionate Person in the universe. He loves being gracious, and slow to anger. He is merciful, forgiving, truthful, and faithful.

> "Remember, O Lord, Your tender mercies and Your lovingkindnesses, for they are from of old."
> Psalm 25:6

God revealed His nature to Moses and then maneuvered the prophet to ask Him the one question He was longing to answer. God wanted Moses to be serious about Him; He wanted to share why Moses should love Him. God is wrapped up in being who He is – He knows what He loves about Himself. He loves being gracious and compassionate and extending mercy. He loves pouring out grace. Moses, He said, this is all yours. This is the list of My qualities which I will reveal to you over the coming months and years. What God shares about Himself is meant for us to experience.

be Thou my vision

What is your vision of God? How you see Him is how you see yourself. It determines how you view your life, your church, even the events that are going on in the Body of Christ. If you fail to see Jesus as your Prince of

Peace, that may be why you cannot find any rest. Seeing Him as your personal Prince of Peace means you're not allowed to worry any more; peace and worry simply can't co-exist. The way we live is profoundly shaped by our image of God.

Are you a sinner who struggles in the love of God, or are you a lover of God who occasionally struggles with sin? How do you see yourself? The more you have the wrong picture of God, the more religious and legalistic you may become. Modern Pharisees are people who do not know who God is for them. They don't understand the nature of God. They don't live in His compassion or mercy. They live by a rulebook, and lose sight of what He is really like, much like the Pharisees in Jesus' time. They couldn't recognize who Jesus was, or His revelation of the Father. "If you have seen Me, you have seen the Father," Jesus tried to explain. "The Father and I are one and the same." Even when He performed signs and wonders, a historic way of recognizing God, they couldn't figure it out.

> "Behold, He who keeps Israel shall neither slumber nor sleep."
> Psalm 121:4

We must see God as our provider, or we will always be anxious about our needs being met. Every time we are in need, it should be an adventure because we are not intimidated; instead, we should be fascinated about what God might do. We must believe He is our provider and become intrigued by how He might meet our needs.

Is He the God who gives us His own life and character? If we're in conflict, we must view the fruit of the Holy Spirit as His provision for the integrity of our lifestyle. There is a whole bundle of God's nature we can draw upon when we are in conflict.

an active God

God is not passive in our circumstances, but active on our behalf. We cannot be resigned to our situations – we must be constantly looking for the power of God to break through. Many of us have just learned to put up with things; the western world is completely passive to the things of God. We put up with all kinds of nonsense in our culture, our society, our communities, and our families. When our backs are against the wall, we should fight with everything in us. Instead, when our backs are against the wall, we wither. We must not become resigned to the situations around us; we must constantly look for the power of God to break through for us.

> "So shall they fear the name of the LORD from the west, and His glory from the rising of the sun; when the enemy comes in like a flood, the Spirit of the LORD will lift up a standard against him."
> Isaiah 59:19

What is your perception of God when you pray? Is He inclining His ear toward you, or do you feel as though you have to persuade Him, or trick Him, into listening? If your image of God is that He is interested and delighted in you, your whole prayer life and approach to Him will be changed. You'll love prayer! For many Christians, prayer is a chore, something we have to do in order to get our weekly allowance from God. Our view of Him is so skewed that we cannot come to Him properly. When distortions creep into our picture of God, the negative effects are felt in every part of our life. Those issues ripple through our relationships, values, ethics, integrity, love, joy, and peace. It affects our righteousness and purity.

We need to reflect wisely upon our image of the Lord's nature. What is it that God wants to be to you in this current season of your life? That is the question we must have an answer to. We must know what it is the Holy Spirit wants to upgrade in our life. Every test, every conflict we face in the months following the upgrade will test us on those breakthroughs. God is not punishing us when things go wrong; troubles don't arise because He can't protect us. God will not reject us, even if we're not perfect. When we do well, God approves of us. When we do poorly, God accepts us. He is compassionate either way. The love of God is never less than 100 percent; He just doesn't know how to be otherwise. He is unchanging and consistent. He takes joy in the fact that He is the Lord and that He never changes. He is the same yesterday, today, and forever; we can be confident of who He is for us.

God's kindness

I have tried to prove the previous paragraph wrong.
There have been times in my walk with the Lord when I
have been downright, deliberately disobedient and God
has still blessed me. I remember one particular occasion
when I just couldn't stand it anymore – His blessing
was making me angry.

"Why are You doing this?" I demanded. "I'm being
rebellious and You keep blessing me! What's wrong
with You?"

When I got quiet, He answered me. "This is what I'm
like – live with it," He said. "I'm not going to change,
I'm always going to be like this. I like being like this, so
live with it." His grace broke the power of sin in me.

Can our hearts be won by God's grace and kindness?
It's an interesting question, isn't it? Too often, we close
ourselves off from the goodness of God
because we're so depressed about our
own performance as a Christian. Where
does this negativity originate?

One day, I was walking down my
church's corridor when I saw someone
coming toward me. I asked him how things were going,
expecting the usual, Christianly cliché, "Oh, fine."
Naturally, I got nothing of the sort.

"I'm really depressed," he said glumly. Why me?
I immediately thought. Why did I ask this on a day I

> "But He is unique, and who
> can make Him change?
> And whatever His soul
> desires, that He does."
> Job 23:13

have to get somewhere? Yet the first thing out of my mouth stunned both of us.

"How do you know?" I said. "Who gave you that information?" We weren't talking about clinical depression, but rather someone who was simply down.

"What do you mean?" he replied.

"Who told you that you are depressed?"

"I don't follow," he said, perplexed.

"Well," I forged ahead, "was it your wife who told you?"

"No."

"Was it one of the elders?"

"No."

"Where did you get the information from, then?" I asked.

"I don't know," he answered.

"Well, don't you feel the tiniest bit dumb then – saying you're depressed and not knowing who diagnosed you?"

"Until now, no," he said.

Some of us have minds like a vacuum cleaner – we suck up any old rubbish. The enemy can come and say, "Feel depressed," and we fall into depression. We should probably check these things out before we jump into them. We must always check the source of our information – where does it come from? If the enemy is trying to sell us something, what might God be saying instead? It's easy to listen to the wrong person and end up broken. Maybe what needs to be broken and reshaped is our image of what God wants to be for us. God loves us for who we are right now – the good, the bad, and the ugly. And He also loves us for who we are going to be.

Let's track those negative thoughts down and take them captive, as Paul told us to do. Slap the handcuffs on them. We need to come to a place where we say, "I'm not going to think that way." Holding our thoughts captive is an important part of upgrading our image of God. We learn to say no to the old image we once had, and yes to the image that's unfolding. We can co-operate with the establishment of that new image in our hearts and lives.

> "Indeed, the darkness shall not hide from You, but the night shines as the day; the darkness and the light are both alike to You."
> Psalm 139:12

Ask the Lord to give you a scripture that reflects the nature of God for you during this season. We can build a strong relationship on a biblical foundation. With Abraham, God said He was his shield. With David, God said He was his refuge, fortress and hiding place. We, too, can have a vivid picture of who God wants to be for us.

my snapshot of God

My own picture of God is that He is the kindest Person I have ever met. Almost 14 years ago, God began to give me a revelation of His kindness.

I believe God wants to show each one of us the panorama of His nature. He wants to show you everything. But there is one aspect of His character that He will want to be yours in particular. This is your doorway into His presence. I love the compassion, mercy, integrity, and grace of God – but my access point to Him is always His kindness.

> "But let him who glories glory in this, that he understands and knows Me, that I am the LORD, exercising lovingkindness, judgment, and righteousness in the earth. For in these I delight."
> Jeremiah 9:24

God has been relentlessly kind to me these past 14 years – day in, day out, month in, month out, year in, year out. Every day, the kindness of God has been in my face. I can't get away from it. I can't remember a day in years where there hasn't been some word of God, some act of kindness, to help me. His kindness is relentless – I love that description. I've come to such a place of dependence on the kindness of God that I have an expectation for it every day. Something kind is going to happen to me. I wake up and I wonder what the kindness will be today. It is my image of who He is. That kindness He has shown me makes me want to be kind and generous to others. It carries forward. What is Jesus like to me? This is the Christ that I have personally encountered:

▶ He has an immense, immeasurable and eternal compassion. His compassion is always greater than my sin.

- He is scandalously forgiving. His mercy burns as it destroys shame.
- He has unbounded patience, unending goodness.
- His love is so compelling ... it heals us. It strips away all our pretense and restores us to happiness.
- His grace is the Empowering Presence within that enables us to feel good about ourselves.
- His mercy is His total favour given gladly to the undeserving heart.
- He is the kindest person I have ever known. His goodness is so outrageous and shocking ... it is actually disreputable to the religious minded.
- He is the happiest person I know, He has the sunniest disposition.
- He is enthusiastically fervent in His pursuit of us.
- He is amazingly humble and gentle but also a powerful warrior king who loves to fight and who laughs at His enemies.
- He has a fabulous servant spirit, needing no title, status or position but joyfully sets an example of simple heartwarming slavery.
- His love is enthralling. It captivates and commands us to be the same.
- His love is designed to overwhelm all things especially fear, shame, low self-esteem.
- He loves being trusted. He is delighted and astonished when we use our faith.
- He will *never* keep a record of our sins or failings.

▶ He has mercy that can never be properly understood or articulated ... just experienced! The only way we can explain mercy is by being merciful ourselves!

▶ Jesus the Redeemer gives us value in the eyes of the Father.

▶ He sees and speaks to our potential. He both protects us and releases us to fulfill all that he wants us to see and know about ourselves.

the disciples' view of God

In Matthew 16:13–20, we learn a lot about how the disciples perceived Jesus. Let's look at the story:

"When Jesus came into the region of Caesarea Philippi, He asked His disciples, saying, 'Who do men say that I, the Son of Man, am?'

So they said, 'Some say John the Baptist, some Elijah, and others Jeremiah or one of the prophets.'

He said to them, 'But who do you say that I am?'

Simon Peter answered and said, 'You are the Christ, the Son of the living God.'

Jesus answered and said to him, 'Blessed are you, Simon Bar-Jonah, for flesh and blood has not revealed this to you, but My Father who is in heaven. And I also say to you that you are Peter, and on this rock I will build My church, and the gates of Hades shall not prevail against it. And I will give you the keys of the kingdom of heaven, and whatever you bind on earth will be bound in heaven, and whatever you loose on earth will be loosed in heaven.'

Then He commanded His disciples that they should tell no one that He was Jesus the Christ."

At least four distorted images of God were expressed by the disciples – the men who knew Jesus best – in this passage: You're John the Baptist, Elijah, Jeremiah, one of the prophets. The one man who put it all together, who upgraded his image of God, was Simon Peter. The instant he did, God announced His call on Peter's life: "On this rock, I will build My church." Peter's perception of

> "He shall receive blessing from the LORD, and righteousness from the God of his salvation."
> Psalm 24:5

God changed, and it would carry him through the trials and tribulations of the next season of his life.

Who do you say that I am? This question strikes at the very heart of our relationship with God. Who do you say that I am? Who is God for you? Have you confessed and proclaimed who God is? Have you declared His role in your life?

God doesn't have identity crises – and He doesn't want you to have them either. His nature must shape who we are. Who do you say that I am? It's time for us to answer that question. Having the right picture of

Conquering Fear

My dear one, you are not in the grip of fear but in the hands of love itself.

Fear of man, fear of the unknown, fear of making mistakes, fear of looking foolish, of trying new things, fear of not being loved, or being good enough.

Fear makes you tense, dark, unable to see things the way I see them.

Let me touch your heart with my perfect, all embracing love and so drive out all your fears.

This next season is about your journey into the heart of my love for you.

I need you to turn your back on fear and face up to my love. We are not battling fear, we are embracing the love that is always present in every circumstance.

For every fear that has gripped you, my love will overwhelm your heart as you learn to stand before me as a much loved child.

Beloved, it is my desire that you thoroughly enjoy this season of freedom from fear to fully embrace my love.

You will know what it is to stand and live in the perfect love of the Father's heart.

ENJOY THIS! I intend to enjoy you becoming more loving and more intimate with my grace.

The breaking of fear will give you a whole new lease of life.

I'm looking forward to love, every day with you.

God will lead us into blessing, destiny and breakthrough.

It did for Peter. "You are the Christ, the Son of the living God," he said. Jesus probably grinned and winked at him – He loved that answer, as His response indicated. Peter's answer pushed him to a new dimension of faith and calling; it gave him a new focus for his ministry. And Jesus prophesied that the entire church would be built on Peter's revelation that Jesus is the Son of God. God builds the church upon the image we have of Him. That view is the very bedrock of our authority.

conclusion

Confidence in God comes when we understand two things: who He is, and who we are. I don't mind the spiritual warfare that surrounds my life because I have such a clear understanding and love for the kindness of God. I actually enjoy the struggle, because I know He wants to be kind to me. Everything I face is just a tool for God to use to show me more of His kind nature. The right image of God opens Heaven to us. Hell itself cannot overcome a man or woman who carries the right image of God in their spirit.

When God sent Moses to Egypt to duel with Pharaoh, he gave specific instructions: "Thus says the LORD: 'Israel is My son, My firstborn. So I say to you, let My son go that he may serve Me. But if you refuse to let him go, indeed I will kill your son, your firstborn'" (Exodus 4:22-23). But while Moses worked Pharaoh, God went behind the scenes and hardened the king's heart, whispering to him, "Don't listen to him." One could forgive Moses for thinking: "Please, stop helping me, Lord."

God hardened Pharaoh's heart because He had an agenda. God wanted to show His power to Israel's enemies. He wanted to teach His people about faithfulness, covenant and perseverance. He had to – the journey to the Promised Land was going to be a grueling one, and the Israelites had to learn to trust God completely.

I cannot overstate the confidence that comes from knowing who God wants to be for us. Just as Jesus prophesied that His church would be built on Peter's revelation of the Son of God, so every single church on earth today is built on its people's perception of who God is for them. Churches must have a corporate image of what God wants for their community. Too many churches don't know what their identity is in Christ, but they desperately need that authority.

> "Behold, I will bring it health and healing; I will heal them and reveal to them the abundance of peace and truth."
> Jeremiah 33:6

Our expectation of God increases when we have the right image of God in our heart. Where are you, right now, in your journey with God? Do you need a breakthrough this year into a different level of relationship with Him? Maybe you are coming into a new level of authority, ministry, or anointing. Take time to upgrade your relationship with God. Perhaps you're disillusioned right now. Maybe you feel burned out or cynical. Your recovery is only available through Christ, and through who Christ wants to be to you. That is your starting point; humans don't have a right to be hurt – we have a right to be healed.

What is it that God wants to be to you this year? What adventure are you going to have with Him? What is it that God wants to show you? What is He longing in His heart to show you? God has a desire for you, and you alone. He knows what He wants to be for you, and He wants to reveal it to you. He wants to lead you through experience after experience as you learn His nature. He wants you to find His truth in joy and difficulty; in pleasure and pain. God will establish who He wants to be for you.

We don't need to worry about how this revelation will come, we just need to co-operate with Him fully. It's all we can offer Him, and it's all that He wants. Who do you say that I am?

upgrades

God does not live in a box; He has no predetermined flight plan, no processes set in stone, as to how He upgrades His relationships with His children. His love for us is completely unique and individual. However, we have learned from the Bible that there are things that God is attracted to; things He loves to be a part of. With that in mind, we offer these 10 steps as a guide to help you upgrade your perspective of God for the next season of your life.

1. Thanksgiving

We enter His gates with thanksgiving ... what are you thankful for? What has God given you? What gifts has He lavished upon you? Take some time and offer Him a heartfelt psalm of thanksgiving, focusing on the blessings He has given you.

If your current circumstances are difficult or hard, what can you be thankful for in terms of God's heart toward you? That He said; "He would never leave nor forsake you" is worthy of thanks alone.

2. Worship

Adore God. Magnify His name. Tell Him of His wondrous deeds. Praise Him for His great majesty. If thanksgiving opens His gates, then worship opens His heart. Don't rush ... just worship Him, in spirit and in truth.

To magnify has two meanings. Firstly to see something bigger than it is in actual size. Secondly to see something as big as it really is. We tend to magnify our problems and not the Lord. See Him as big as He is.

3. Stillness

It is in stillness and peace that God begins to speak. Remember, His voice wasn't in the whirlwind or the thunder, it was still and quiet. Be still and know that He is God. Rest there. Live there. Connect with the Almighty there. Still the clamoring in your thoughts. We all have a background conversation in our minds that either feeds our fears or lifts our spirits. Stillness promotes a God consciousness.

4. See Him as your Prince of Peace

Embrace God as your Prince of Peace, draw on His restful nature to sustain you. As troubles rise in your heart, ask the Prince of Peace to soothe you. He is your refuge, your strong tower. If it helps, picture a strong tower, ruled by God. Live in it.

5. See Him as your Man of War

God is also your protector; paradoxically, He is gentle as a Lamb, and fierce as a Lion. He is your shield, your sword, your strength. Let Him fight your battles for you ... don't take matters into your own hands. Allow Him to be fully God in your life – the provider of peace, and the protector of your life.

6. Examine your new season

Tell God what you are coming into. Share your fears, your dreams. Hide nothing – He knows and sees all anyway. Listen as He whispers to you.

Expect the Lord to give you "a spirit of wisdom and revelation in the knowledge of Him" (Ephesians 1:17).

7. What does He want to teach you?

Begin to ask God questions. What does He want to teach you in this next season of life that He could only teach you this way? What lessons are there for you to learn? What must you travel through on this next leg of your journey together? What pitfalls does He want you to avoid? What will you be tested on? What glory does He want to bestow on you?

It is important at least that you write your questions down and develop an expectation that God will answer them. The revelation that comes will lead you into a new experience of Him.

8. What does He want to be for you?

Now ask Him what He wants to be for you. Knowing where you are headed, He has a plan to reveal something new and fresh about himself to you. What is it? What is God like? What does He have for you? Take your time ... patience may be one of things He wants to show you.

He will give you a vision of all that He wants to be for you. Your circumstances will then be filled with promise. You will perceive every problem as an opportunity to experience all that God longs to be for you.

9. Ask Him for those things

Remembering everything the two of you have shared over the past several minutes, ask Him for all of it. Ask Him to be more real to you than ever. Be specific – you may want to craft a written prayer emphasizing God's desires for you. Ask for everything that Heaven holds for you.

Write a reply to God detailing what your responses will be to each situation that is under adjustment.

10. Abide in Him

Just be. Don't rush out. Don't be panicked. Just be with Him. In the Garden of Eden, God and Adam would sit and talk with one another. Neither had anywhere else they'd rather be. Live in God. Abide in Him. Love Him. Minister to Him. Just be.

your picture of God

Answer as many questions as you need to!

▶ What is your current picture of God? Write it down in 4–6 sentences or phrases.

▶ How long have you had this image? Is it time for an upgrade?

▶ Is your image biblical? Can you put scripture(s) alongside it? Do so!

▶ What do you need to change?

▶ What do you need God to be to you in this current season?

▶ Sit quietly, relax and ask the Holy Spirit to give you a vision of God for this next season. Keep persevering until the whole picture emerges *and* your faith begins to rise and worship flows.

▶ What scripture can support this image?

▶ What is the Spirit saying to you through this picture and the word?

▶ How can you become this image of God to the people around you? What must change in you?

▶ Now keep this picture alive through praise and worship!

developing your relationship with God in a new season of calling

Answer the following questions as you meditate on what it is God wants to show you during the next season of your life.

1. What are you moving into? A new season, calling, revelation, response, role, or something else?

2. What could this situation show you about God that couldn't happen through another means?

3. Right now, what is it that the Lord wants to do *in you* that will enable you to occupy this new place for Him in the spirit?

4. What is it that the Lord wants to be *through you* for the people around you?

5. Given that our spiritual maturity arises out of our knowledge of the ways of God, what are the likely situations/people, both positive and negative, that God may use to develop (3) and (4) above?

6. At the end of this season, how do you think your upgraded relationship with God will impact your effectiveness in ministry?

an inheritance word for this season

In the context of our relationship with God there are times when He asks us a direct question that connects His desire for us with our longings for Him.

He spoke to Solomon, *"Ask what you wish me to do for you"* (1 Kings 3:5). With Ahaz, His approach was similar though more poetic. *"Ask a sign for yourself from the LORD your God; make it deep as Sheol or high as heaven"* (Isaiah 7:11).

Jesus asked the question *"What do you want Me to do for you?"* (Matthew 20:32). Though the background of this situation was healing we do understand in Christ that all the interventions of God are relational in context. Jesus was fully aware of the Father's real pleasure in giving us the Kingdom (Luke 12:32).

"Every good gift comes down from the Father of lights" said James (1:17) ... so be wise in what you ask for! (4:3).

When asking God to upgrade your image of Him, it is important to ask for an inheritance word. These are pieces of the Bible that He brings to your attention and asks you to meditate on for long periods of time. As a son or daughter of the Almighty, you have an inheritance, and God wants you to know what it is. Jesus Himself, after spending 40 days and 40 nights being tested in the wilderness (see Luke 4), returned to civilization and went straight to a synagogue. He opened the Scriptures to Isaiah 61 and proclaimed it as His inheritance. *"Today, this word is fulfilled in your hearing,"* He said.

I love receiving inheritance words, as they reveal to me what it is God wants to be for me in the next season of my life. He will often wrap the upgraded view we need to have of Him into a poignant piece of Scripture. Our job is to seek those verses out and get everything we can out of them. Then we must apply them to our lives during that new season.

God will give you an inheritance word, if He hasn't done so already. The word will set you up to discover what you're going to experience during the next stage of your journey of faith. It may be two or three passages of the Bible, but He will put it in your heart, and it is your inheritance. Ask for it. When you receive a passage, don't read anything else for a while. Read it and re-read it. Memorize it, if you can. Take it apart, piece by piece. Study it. Look it up in Bible commentaries. Research the original language. Ask God to illuminate His truth in it. *Every ounce of revelation is yours to experience.* This passage is part of the conversation in Heaven about you, so use it for all it's worth. Then write a crafted prayer about it, asking for the things that have been laid out as promises in your inheritance word.

[See the *Certainty of Prayer Interactive Journal* for more on crafted prayer and inheritance words.]

This is one of the most classic songs about the love of God that I have ever heard. Written by my friend Joe King it never fails to move me.

I Will always Love You [1]

I loved you long before you met me
And then you gave your life to me
But should one day you turn and walk away
I will always love you; I will always love you,
I will always love you; yes I will I always will.

My love will never cease towards you
But should I have a change of heart
It is because my heart has ceased to beat
I will always love you; I will always love you,
I will always love you; yes I will I always will.

When all around you seems in darkness
When you have plumbed right to the depths
No pit is so deep I'm not deeper still
I will always love you; I will always love you,
I will always love you; yes I will I always will.

And when the day has almost ended
When evening comes and walls you in
When there is no one else to comfort you
I will always love you; I will always love you,
I will always love you; yes I will I always will.

[1] *I Will Always Love You* from the album *Next To You* available through www.joekinguk.com – used with permission

Here are my arms for you to cling to
Here are my wounds where you can hide
Here are the tears that I have cried for you
I will always love you; I will always love you,
I will always love you; yes I will I always will.

My love is constant as the sunrise
As changeless as the stars of night
My child, as sure as the returning tide
I will always love you; I will always love you,
I will always love you; yes I will I always will.

Joe King contact details:
    joekinguk@aol.com
    www.joeking.com

FAQ:
frequently asked questions

Q. *Who is Graham Cooke and how can I find more information about him?*

A. Graham Cooke is a speaker and author who splits his time between Southampton, England, and Vacaville, California. He has been involved in prophetic ministry since 1974. He founded and directed The School of Prophecy, which has received international acclaim for its advanced series of in-depth training programs. Graham is a member of Community Church in Southampton (UK), and is part of c.net (Cornerstone) team. He is married to Heather, and they have three children, Ben, Seth and Sophie. You can learn more about Graham at www.grahamcooke.com or by writing him, PO Box 91, Southampton, England, SO15 57E.

Q. *How can I become a prayer partner with Graham?*

A. Check his website, www.grahamcooke.com, for all of the information you need.

Q. *Has Graham written any other books?*

A. Graham has written two other books, *A Divine Confrontation ... Birth Pangs of the New Church* (Destiny Image) and *Developing Your Prophetic Gifting* (Sovereign World).

Both are available at most Christian bookstores or at www.grahamcooke.com.

about the author

Graham Cooke is married to Heather, and they have three adult offspring, Ben, Seth, and Sophie. Graham and Heather divide their time between Southampton, England, and Vacaville, California.

Graham is a member of the apostolic team of c.net (Cornerstone), a network of ministries and a family of churches spanning 44 nations. He is a member of Community Church in Southampton (UK), responsible for the prophetic and training program, and working with team leader Billy Kennedy. In California, he is part of the pastoral leadership team, working with senior pastor David Crone. He has responsibility for Insight, a training program within the church and for the region.

Graham is a popular conference speaker and is well known for his training programs on the prophetic, spiritual warfare, intimacy with God, leadership, and spirituality. He functions as a consultant within c.net (and beyond), specifically helping churches make the transition from one dimension of calling to a higher level of vision and ministry. He has a passion to build prototype churches that can fully reach our postmodern society.

A strong part of Graham's ministry is in producing finances and resources to help the poor, supporting many projects around the world. He also financially supports and helps to underwrite church planting, leadership development, evangelism, and health and rescue projects in the third world. If you wish to become a financial partner for the sake of missions, please contact Graham's office where his personal assistant, Carole Shiers, will be able to assist you.

Graham has many prayer partners who play a significant part in his ministry. For more information, check his website.

Contact details for Graham Cooke:

- **United States:** Vaca Valley Christian Life Center, 6391 Leisure Town Road, Vacaville, CA 95687, USA
  email: FUTURETRAININGINST@prodigy.net

- **United Kingdom:** Sword of Fire Ministries, PO Box 1, Southampton, SO16 7WJ
  email: admin@swordfire.org.uk

- **Canada:** Jenny Bateman, Friends at Langley Vineyard, 5708 Glover Road, Langley, BC, V3A 4H8
  email: jenn@shopvineyard.com

- *Website*: http://www.grahamcooke.com